BACKYARD ANIMALS

CARDINALS

by Genevieve Nilsen

TABLE OF CONTENTS

tadpole books

WORDS TO KNOW

beak

eggs

feathers

female

male

nest

CARDINALS

I see a red bird!

It is a male cardinal.

It has black around its beak.

This is a female.

It is red and tan.

feathers

Feathers keep it warm.

It finds food.

The nest is in a tree.

The eggs have spots!

They sing.

Chirp! Chirp!

LET'S REVIEW!

We can tell if a cardinal is a male or female by its colors. Is this cardinal a male or female? How can you tell?

INDEX